GLADIATORS
£4.99
UK only

GLADIATORS FAN CLUB

If you would like to join the official
Gladiators Fan Club,
write for details to:
PO Box 252,
Bexley
Kent
DA5 1JU

Published in Great Britain by
World International,
an imprint of Egmont Publishing Ltd.,
Egmont House, PO Box 111,
Great Ducie Street,
Manchester M60 3BL.
Printed in Italy.
ISBN 0-7498-2019-5

Written by Rob Holden
Edited by John Malam
Designed by Viv Harper

NOTE – PLAY SAFELY!

Gladiators and contenders have undergone considerable training – do not attempt to imitate their actions or recreate Gladiator events.

CONTENTS

LET BATTLE COMMENCE...

Welcome to the 1995 Gladiators Annual. We hope you enjoy all the profiles, the fascinating behind-the-scenes features and the fabulous photos.

The response to our last Annual was terrific and we'd like to take this opportunity to thank all of you who wrote in to us – *we've included some of your comments in this year's Annual*.

Don't forget to enter our great competition on page 60 – you could win a brilliant bicycle or a selection of Gladiators games!

Right now, we can't wait to get stuck into the next bunch of contenders, in the most exciting, the most challenging competition on TV...GLADIATORS!

Keep watching...keep safe...and...
LET BATTLE COMMENCE!

GLADIATORS

COBRA

After the 1993 Gladiators Celebrity Special, Cobra was extremely critical of one particular guest – Wimbledon soccer star, Vinny Jones. *'Vinny said the celebrity contestants were well fit, and not just guys off the street,'* Cobra recalls. *'Well, let me tell you, the "guys" he was referring to – the normal Gladiators' contenders – are all very good athletes in their own right. And I wouldn't fancy his chances against any of them!'*

This kind of reaction underlines just how serious the Gladiators are about their show and the contestants who brave the arena throughout the series. And it demonstrates the kind of commitment we've come to expect from the lethal Cobra.

Before joining the Gladiators, Cobra had already been a dedicated amateur boxer and body-building champion in London and his native Kent.

His work as a labourer helped to keep him fit. *'And it was great fun too, 'cause it involved demolishing buildings!'*

Being a big fan of American Gladiators, Cobra applied to be a contender in the British version. *'But for some reason, the producers asked me to try out as an actual Gladiator,'* he says. *'I successfully did what was asked and duly became Cobra, a name I carry with pride, vigour and enthusiasm.'*

"He helps with charity work and he is the best tough Gladiator."
Matthew Haines, aged 7, Yeovil

"He's a snake in the grass with a deadly bite!"
Heather Stancliffe, aged 13, Middlesbrough

COBRA FACTS

Height:	6ft
Weight:	15st
Vital Stats:	Chest 50in, waist 32in, thigh 26in, arm 18.5in
Birthdate:	29 October 1963
Starsign:	Scorpio
Birthplace:	Dartford, Kent
Present Home:	Belvedere, Kent

LIKES AND DISLIKES

Cobra's favourite Gladiators event is Danger Zone: *'Because it's easy and a lot of fun to shoot at the contestants.'*

But he dislikes The Wall. *'It's so physically demanding, and the short time in which we have to film a show gives you very little time to recuperate.'*

THE GAMES part 1

DANGER ZONE

The contender, armed with a missile launcher, has to reach four 'safe stations' and de-fuse them within ten seconds, before they auto-destruct. Meanwhile, a Gladiator stands on a high platform firing tennis balls at the contender – at the speed of a Wimbledon tennis champion! Contenders must fire their missile at a target above the Gladiator's head. The contender either loses if hit – or wins by reaching the final safe station.

Points: *10 for hitting the target above the Gladiator, 5 for hitting the target below the Gladiator – or 1 point for each safe station reached.*

SUSPENSION BRIDGE

One minute of absolute suspense. Gladiator and contender, each carrying a huge hammer head, begin at either end of the Suspension Bridge and meet to slug it out somewhere near the middle. Pushing is not allowed. Any combatant removed from the bridge or knocked to their knees for five seconds loses the contest.

Points: *10 for knocking the Gladiator off the bridge, 5 for a drawn contest.*

TILT

You need a head for heights and a heightened sense of balance to play Tilt! Gladiator and contender are joined at the waist by a long rope which stretches from one Tilt Platform to the other. Two 30-second tug o'war pulls determine the winner.

Points: *5 for each 'pull' providing the Gladiator is dislodged. A draw is deemed a 'loss'.*

SKYTRAK

An upside-down chase on a suspended track. Two Gladiators chase two contenders trying to catch them before they reach the finish line. Gladiators attempt to strike contenders' detonators and explode their backpacks.

Points: *10 for first contender home, 5 for second. No points awarded if caught by a Gladiator.*

POWERBALL

One minute in which to score as many goals as possible. Sounds easy? Don't you believe it! Two contenders attempt to place either red or blue balls into any of the five basket-like goals. Three Gladiators try to stop them!

Points: *3 for each ball placed inside the centre goal, 2 for each ball placed within any of the four outer goals.*

SWINGSHOT

It's all-action as a contender swings on a shock cord towards a three-coloured pole studded with coloured balls – and guarded by two Gladiators! The contender attempts to grab a ball and return it to his or her pod. The higher the ball gathered, the more points scored.

Points: *1 per yellow ball grabbed, 2 per blue ball, 3 per red ball.*

HANG-TOUGH

Aerial action played out on 60 rings spaced four feet apart and suspended 12 feet above the arena floor. Contenders attempt to swing across the rings to reach the Gladiators' platform. Reasonably easy, you might think – except for a Gladiator determined to ensure the contender never reaches the target!

Points: *10 for a successful crossing, 5 for 'Hanging-Tough' in the scoring zone.*

DID YOU KNOW?

Before Gladiators is recorded at the National Indoor Arena in Birmingham, it takes two weeks to set up all the elaborate staging and lighting. Meanwhile the contenders will be undergoing two weeks of intense training in all the events!

The fifteen shows in a Gladiators series – eight heats, four quarter-finals, two semi-finals and the final – are recorded over a two-week period, interspersed with days off for the Gladiators!

Two Gladiator shows are recorded in a day. One in the afternoon, the other in the evening. It takes approximately four hours to record each one!

Twelve cameras are used to shoot Gladiators. This includes two cameras mounted on a movable Technocrane. Four operatives are needed to work each Technocrane!

Once a show has been recorded, it take two days to edit out all the stops and starts, put in all the graphic effects and get the timing of the show exactly right!

Reserve contenders stand-by during the shooting of the early heats. If a contender is forced to pull out of a semi-final or the final, then the next highest loser takes their place!

A children's version of Gladiators is currently being planned. It will be based on physiological, fitness and health competitions, rather than the direct confrontational events in the grown-ups' version. The adult Gladiators *will* be involved!

An astonishing 14.5 million viewers regularly tune in to Gladiators!

FALCON

STALKING HER PREY!

Gladiators' fans are always recognising Falcon in the street and asking her for her autograph. *'It just means that shopping takes a lot longer,'* she says. *'In fact, I have very little time for myself these days as I'm very busy doing personal appearances and teaching aerobics. But it doesn't bother me at all – I love being a Gladiator and wouldn't change it for anything!'*

Falcon also finds time for keeping fit. *'I train with weights four times a week and do aerobics whenever I can.'* Before entering body-building competitions she goes on a special diet. *'It consists of lean chicken, fish, baked potatoes, pasta, rice, vegetables and fruit – but my favourite food of all is pizza!'*

In the arena Falcon really lives up to her name by stalking her prey on her favourite events – Powerball, Atlaspheres and Hang-Tough. But she admits to disliking Tilt. *'It gives so much advantage to the contender,'* she explains. *'The Gladiator has to get his or her Tilt board back quickly if he or she is to stand any chance of winning.'*

As if to underline just how tough Gladiators is, Falcon recalls a scary moment from the 1993 series: *'During Powerball, Zodiac and a contender collided and were both unconscious for a minute. Zodiac had to go off, but the contender continued with the game. Just before the whistle went she was facing me and she made the sign of the cross. I felt worried as I didn't want to further her injuries.'*

"She is strong and graceful, like the bird she represents."
Katy Jones, aged 10, Much Hadham, Herts

"She's a lovely lady, and she's pretty too!"
Andrew Smith, aged 9, Tilbury, Essex

FALCON FACTS

Height:	5ft 7.5in
Weight:	10st 7lbs
Vital Stats:	38-24-34
Birthdate:	6 November 1963
Starsign:	Scorpio
Birthplace:	Brighton
Present Home:	Basingstoke

OFF DUTY!

Falcon loves to relax by reading, walking or listening to music. *'I like all kinds of music – depending on my mood,'* she says. Her favourite TV programme is *Blind Date*, and her favourite movie is *The Fugitive*, starring Harrison Ford.

IT'S ALL IN THE STARS

HUNTER

"For someone so young, he is so strong."
James Scott, aged 6, Epsom

Gemini-born Hunter always checks-out his horoscope to see what life has in store for him. A couple of years ago, when he was working as a printer, we reckon his stars must have read something like 'A big change is about to come your way' – because it was around that time that Nigel Lythgoe spotted his picture in a magazine after he'd won the Junior North East Britain Body-Building title.

Nigel invited Hunter to try out for the series! *'I did the test and passed,'* he says. *'Two hours later I was "Hunter" and sitting in on a meeting with thirteen other Gladiators!'*

Since then Hunter hasn't looked back and has thoroughly enjoyed the experience of being a Gladiator. *'I love meeting all the fans,'* he says. *'I travel around all over the country, seeing new places, meeting new people, making new friends – and I even appeared in panto last year which was great.'*

In the Gladiators' arena, Hunter really makes his mark in the power events. *'Because of my power-lifting, I'm one of the strongest Gladiators. This year I'm even better because I've trained specifically to be a Gladiator, whereas last year I was chosen so late and couldn't train properly. This time I intend to be the best!'*

"He's young and sexy!"
Anna Simpson, aged 12, Kings Lynn

HUNTER FACTS

Height:	6ft 3in
Weight:	18st
Vital Stats:	Chest 51in, waist 33in, arms 19in, leg 28in
Birthdate:	12 June 1973
Starsign:	Gemini
Birthplace:	Beverley, near Hull
Present Home:	York

HUNTER'S MENU

Here is a typical day's food enjoyed by a hungry young Gladiator...

1 Large bowl of porridge and sultanas.

2 Tuna and pasta salad *('Mixed with tomatoes – yum!')*

3 Large fruit salad

4 Protein drink

5 2 chicken breasts, potato and vegetables

6 5 egg whites

'And for a treat, I love Italian food and flapjacks!'

JOHN FASHANU – ALWAYS ON THE BALL!

John Fashanu is one of Britain's top footballers. A striker of immense power, he has been a mainstay of Wimbledon's 'crazy gang' team for the past eight years.

Having previously played for Norwich City, Crystal Palace, Lincoln City and Millwall, he joined the Dons in March 1986 in a £125,000 transfer deal.

John's arrival at Wimbledon had an immediate effect and his goals helped to secure promotion for the club from the Second Division to the First where they have remained a much respected force ever since.

In 1988 John was a member of the Dons' side which beat mighty Liverpool 1–0 in the greatest FA Cup Final upset of all time.

The following season saw him make his international debut for England against Chile, at Wembley. A few days later he wore the No. 9 shirt in a 2–0 away victory over Scotland. Many soccer pundits reckon he should have been called up for international duty on many more occasions.

With his outgoing personality, the articulate John Fashanu has, among other things, undertaken fund-raising work for the aged, set up a soccer school for under-privileged Sowetan children in Johannesburg and been a tireless worker against apartheid (for which he received a United Nations citation).

John is something of a martial arts expert. He is the proud holder of a black belt in Sam-tu-dang and also practises Tai-chi and Wing Chung Kung Fu.

And he has crafted a more than promising career for himself in the media. He has appeared many times on TV, in such shows as *Surprise, Surprise*, *A Question of Sport*, *Tonight with Jonathan Ross* and *You Bet!*

But his biggest non-footballing role has been as co-presenter of Gladiators...

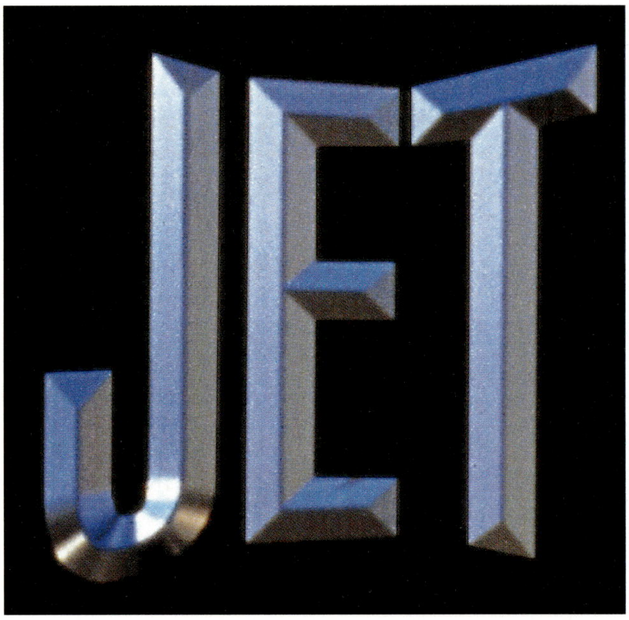

With the supreme confidence that Jet displays in the Gladiators' arena, it is hard to believe that she was once a shy and shrinking violet. *'When I was 16 I experienced something of a crisis of confidence. I wanted to be thin, but I thought I was ugly, muscular and large – when of course I wasn't,'* she recalls.

It was an interest in gymnastics that had initially started Jet in pursuit of the body beautiful. Inspired by the Russian Olympic gold medallist Olga Korbut, the future Gladiator blossomed at the sport, becoming a member of the junior British squad, and the North of England Junior Champion from 1973 to 1983.

As a teenager Jet moved into dance and drama. She describes her first job as *'a real break'* which came while she was studying drama in London. *'It was a musical revue in which we did numbers from Grease, Sweet Charity and other terrific shows. I was 18 and it earned me my Equity card well before I graduated. It was fabulous being paid to entertain!'*

After that she appeared many times on stage, TV and in film before becoming 'Jet'.

The Gladiators connection came about after she had been favourably featured in a fitness publication. *'The casting director for Gladiators called me in for a meeting, followed by fitness trials. But I imagined I was not be big enough to qualify as a Gladiator – so I was pleasantly surprised when I became "Jet".'*

Becoming a Gladiator has opened many doors for Jet...and one of them could lead to YOUR school. *'I want readers to know that I visit schools and colleges with my creative, educational and inspiring Funk & Fitness workshop and lecture for 11- to 18-year-olds,'* she says. *'Having experienced all sorts of confidence and low self-esteem problems as a young person, I feel I'm now in a good position to help educate youngsters towards making a more confident and less stressful transition into adulthood.'*

"She is pretty and friendly."
Hailey Willson, aged 8, Rayleigh, Essex

"Jet is the best and she can put anyone to the test!"
Jonathan Ball, aged 5, Mansfield

JET FACTS

Height:	5ft 7in
Weight:	9st 5lbs
Vital Stats:	38-24-36
Birthdate:	13 February 1970
Starsign:	Aquarius
Birthplace:	Teeside, Cleveland
Present Homes:	Surrey, York and London

I'M IN A GOOD POSITION TO HELP EDUCATE YOUNGSTERS

LIKES AND DISLIKES

Jet loves The Wall. *'I had a clean record in the event in '93,'* she says. She's also a big fan of Hang-Tough. *'It's so nerve-wracking – but thrilling when you succeed.'* She likes Powerball too, because it's a team event, and Danger Zone because she's usually accurate. Her least favourite event is Joust. *'It takes a lot for me to become really aggressive. I prefer the more calculating events,'* she says.

JET – A DAY IN THE LIFE OF A GLADIATOR

Jet describes a typical day during the recording of Gladiators...

Throughout the recording of Gladiators we all stay in an hotel not far from the National Indoor Arena, in Birmingham. I usually get up at around 8.30 to 9.00am – depending on how late we finished the night before!

After breakfast we all congregate on the 'Gladi-bus' which takes us to the NIA, where my next stop is usually the make-up suite.

After make-up, I get changed and then spend approximately an hour warming-up and preparing my body for the specific events of the day. This is also an important time to 'switch-on' mentally for the job in hand.

We then get our 'call' to go to the back of the set, and from then on it's all nerves and action until two episodes of Gladiators are 'in the can'.

During this time, my head-set stereo comes in handy as I enjoy listening to music – it soothes me, motivates me and focuses my thoughts.

After filming, usually sometime after 11.00pm, we are driven back to our hotel. We're all still mentally wound up at this time and usually sit and relax and wind-down in the lounge. This process is normally aided by pots of tea, coffee – or even a glass of wine! But my favourite is hot chocolate.

Then it's time to bathe in a lovely relaxing bath. I get to bed at around 12.30.

During the filming period all my business and career interests are put on the back burner – complete focus on performing accurately and safely as 'Jet' comes first.

LIGHTNING

When we were putting this annual together, Lightning dropped us a line saying: *'My fans have been complaining that they don't know enough about me. They think I'm a very private, secretive person. A lot of people say I look moody and miserable. All I can say is that if you have to psych yourself up for events like Duel, you can't crack jokes and smile heartily as you'd soon lose your concentration. But really I'm a friendly, happy and polite girl!'*

She says that being a Gladiator has not really changed her as a person. *'I still have the same friends, I still visit the same places. Perhaps other people have changed towards me.'*

Lightning has trained in sports all her life. She started as a gymnast – eventually becoming a member of the British junior squad. She also played rounders and netball and was a prominent member of her school's athletics team. At sixteen, Lightning started weight-training.

In May 1991, after she had competed in the British Body-Building Championship finals, Lightning's photograph appeared in a magazine. Soon afterwards she had a call from the Gladiators production team, inviting her to audition for the show. *'It was my first time in London and I felt nervous being miles from home, but at the same time I was excited about the whole idea.'*

She was eventually asked to go to further trials at the National Indoor Arena in Birmingham. *'I enjoyed those tests and was pleased with my results – especially when I was told they wanted to use me as a reserve.'* But after seeing how well she performed in practice sessions, she was told that she would appear as Lightning in all nine shows of the series. *'I had no idea it would become a full-time occupation. But these days I can't wait for the next series to come along. I'm ready!'*

"She is a good mover and she is good in all events!"
Neil Taylor, aged 10, Mansfield

TRAINING, TRAINING ... AND MORE TRAINING

Nowadays, Lightning does not compete in any sports, except the events in Gladiators, but obviously she keeps herself in tip-top condition. *'Even if I wasn't a Gladiator, I'd be training anyway. But knowing I'm in the public eye, being seen on TV and at public appearances, gives me more incentive to work-out harder and more intensely.'*

LIGHTNING FACTS

Height:	5ft 7in
Weight:	9st 9lbs
Birthdate:	25 December 1971
Starsign:	Capricorn
Birthplace:	Burntwood, Staffs
Present Home:	Rawnsley, Staffs

I DO LIKE TO WIN!
Lightning x

NIGHTSHADE

'*Fast and furious!*' That's the way Nightshade likes her Gladiators events. She revels in the fighting games as they enble her to show her love of competition, her fitness and – especially – her strength.

'I'll always remember my battle on the Suspension Bridge with Pauline Oliver,' Nightshade recalls. *'She was a fine contender who had managed to beat other female Gladiators in the event. We had a great fight. She managed to knock me down – but I got up and she had to "eat mat" when I knocked her off the Bridge. Pauline was gutted because I had beaten her and she promised me the mother of all fights if we should ever meet on the Bridge again.'*

"She is nice, and pretty."
Stuart McKie, aged 7, Isle of Mull

After that epic battle, Shadow and Warrior said that Nightshade had proved that only the very best athletes can be Gladiators.

'I met Pauline again in the semi-finals and I won again – which goes to show that no one should write cheques with their mouth that their body can't cash! The compliments the other Gladiators paid me after that made me sure in my mind that I was amongst fine sports people who provide some of the best sporting entertainment on television.'

All of this means that Nightshade has to keep herself in tip-top condition. *'My favourite ways are climbing, walking, exercising to music and Tai Kwon Do,'* she says.

"She doesn't seem to have any problems at the challenges."
Diane Cowan, aged 10, Darlington

OFF DUTY!

When she's off duty, Nightshade loves nothing more than *'a nice meal with my family and friends. My friends have lovely children, so I also do a lot of babysitting.'* She loves going to the movies too – her favourite recent films were Demolition Man and Made In America.

NIGHTSHADE FACTS

Height:	6ft
Weight:	11st
Vital Stats:	36-27-39
Birthdate:	14 November 1960
Starsign:	Scorpio
Birthplace:	Jamaica
Present Home:	Birmingham

Nightshade

THE BATTLER ON THE BRIDGE!

THE CHALLENGERS

Over 25,000 would-be contenders applied to participate in the third series of Gladiators. That's more than *double* the number who wrote in for the second series.

Each was sent a Contender's Application Form which asks all sorts of questions, about age, occupation, hobbies and interests, best and worst qualities, sporting background, health and fitness, height and weight.

This information was then fed into the Gladiators' computer which considered all the factors and finally came up with some 12,500 people who were invited for try-outs.

Try-outs were held in April 1994 in London, Bournemouth, Cardiff, Belfast, Birmingham, Manchester, Newcastle and Edinburgh. Each applicant had to complete a very stiff test which involved:

- Running 800 metres on a jogging machine (two-and-a-half minutes for men, 3 minutes for women).
- Performing straight-under-arm hanging chin-ups (men 10, women 5), with five seconds between each.

Phil Norman – winner!

Sylene Clarke

- Crossing a horizontal ladder hand over hand.
- Climbing a 20 foot rope (men twice, women once) inside a minute.

Associate Producer Ken Warwick says that only 1% of applicants get through this stage. *'I'd say that 65–70% drop out at the running stage – it's difficult on a running machine anyway. But we have to know if they've got the necessary endurance. Potential contenders must be seriously fit.'*

Next stage for the 'survivors' is a knock-about with pugil sticks. *'We pad them, helmet them and match people of equal weight together,'* says Ken. *'The object of the exercise is not only to see how aggressive they are, or how willing they are to get stuck in – it's actually to see how tolerant they are. It's no good if someone gets a knock, sees red and then goes crazy. We need to know they can take it as well as dish it out!'*

If they get through all of that, applicants then undergo a video interview which assesses their personality. Eventually, 50 probable contenders are selected, from which the final 32 are chosen – together with stand-ins in case of any mishaps.

THE CONTENDERS – roll of honour

Listed here are all the contenders who took place in the first two series of Gladiators.

Series 1 – Men

Winner: WEININGER IRWIN
Runner-up: KYM DALTON
Jonathan Riley
Ludwig Ramsey
Dean Jackson
Jeremy Nelson
Chris Saunders
Roger Allen
Simon Goddard
Stephen Lewis
Tony Bayford
Tracy Harris
Derek Collett
Russell Williams

Jon Morgan

Series 2 – Men

Winner: PHIL NORMAN
Runner-up: BRIAN WARD
Richard Bury
Glenn Webbe
Gary Towers
Roddy Mackay
Stephen Robinson
Alan Bates
Deane Hart
Jon Morgan
Rik Keisewetter
Gary Dodds
Roland Hill
Steve Quick
Tim Anstiss
Chris Yeomans

Stephen Robinson

Series 1 – Women

Winner: VANDA FAIRCHILD
Runner-up: JANE MORRIS
Gabbi Yorath
Moya Lidden
Viviene Rattigan
Jennifer Le Grande
Lisa Morgan
Nicola Bawden
Michelle Brewer
Clare Egerton
Karen Beaumont
Sharon Phillips
Chrissie Mullings
Catherine Haughey

Jon Morgan with Ulrika Jonsson

Series 2 – Women

Winner: JEAN KLENK
Runner-up: GEORGINA BERGER
Katie Tanner
Pauline Oliver
Rhian Prichard
Rowan Duxbury
Mandy Gornicki
Paula Bisley
Helen Williams
Sophie Cheston
Jacqui Thomson
Tracy Johnson
Gail Rickett
Sylene Clarke
Susan Surman
Vicki McCann

PANTHER

I HAD NO IDEA WHAT A GLADIATOR WAS!

"She gives the contenders a run for their money!"
Robert Bortkiewicz, aged 11, Banbury

"She is always smiling and looks like she's having fun!"
Lisa Davis, aged 9, Arran, Scotland

PANTHER FACTS

Height:	5ft 7in
Weight:	10st 7lbs
Vital Stats:	37-24-36
Birthdate:	14 October 1963
Starsign:	Libra
Birthplace:	Blyth, Northumberland
Present Home:	Slough

Panther was already a successful body-builder – Miss Britain, Miss Europe, Miss Universe, Miss Russia – when she was invited on to the *Noel Edmonds Show* to talk about health and fitness. Watching that show was none other than Nigel Lythgoe, a man who knows a potential Gladiator when he sees one!

'Nigel invited me along for an interview,' Panther recalls. *'I had no idea what a Gladiator was at the time, but after visiting LWT and watching videos of the American version, I knew it was a job I wanted. I then did some strength and stamina tests and was asked if I would like the name "Panther". I was thrilled and couldn't wait to get started.'*

Now, three years on, she is recognised wherever she goes *'...no matter what disguise I wear!'*

But she isn't complaining *'It is lovely to be appreciated by all the Gladiators' fans – and it feels good to make them feel good.'*

When we asked Panther if there's anything special she would like the readers of this book to know, she had no hesitation in telling us: *'Yes, I went to Florida with my fiancé, Sean, in March, and we were married there.'*

DID YOU KNOW...

Panther recently opened a new gym and fitness centre in Uxbridge, Middlesex. *'It's the biggest and best in the country,'* she says proudly. *'We have experts in all fields of fitness and physique. People can start getting fit, or increase their fitness alongside Gladiators such as Cobra, Scorpio and me!'*

FABULOUS FANS

'We really love our fans,'* says Jet. *'Gladiators just wouldn't be the same without them. They help create an exciting, vibrant atmosphere and they mean everything to us!'

JOHN ANDERSON – he's in charge!

No one – not even Wolf, howling at his fiercest – can ever pull the wool over John Anderson's eyes! He's the man in the black-and-white striped shirt. The man with the rulebook, the whistle and the stopwatch. The man whose word is law as far as Gladiators' events are concerned – he's the referee!

'During a tournament, I control the events and ensure that Gladiators and contenders stick to the rules,' he says. *'If there's an infringement of any kind, I have to use my judgement to decide what should happen. And I'm the one who officially awards the points.'*

All of this requires the utmost concentration, as every Gladiators' event is played out at lightning speed. If a dispute arises, then John will refer to the video evidence.

But there is a lot more to his job than that. *'I'm also the Director of Training, and I teach the contenders the rules of the games and arrange practice time for them.'*

John, an experienced athletics coach, has nothing but admiration for Gladiators and contenders. *'It's all high-level performance by people who want to do well for reasons of pride and achievement. There is so much tension in the air when the cameras roll.'*

THE GAMES part 2

THE WALL

This one literally drives contenders up the wall! They have 60 seconds to climb 36 feet up a wall studded with grips. Unfortunately, ten seconds after the men and women begin, a Gladiator gives chase. Many Gladiators admit this is the scariest of all the events.
Points: *10 for succesfully climbing The Wall, 5 for remaining on The Wall.*

GAUNTLET

Speed is of the essence as contenders have just 30 seconds in which to cover a 60 foot alleyway. Five Gladiators do their utmost to stop them, using ramrods.
Points: *10 for the fastest completed running of the Gauntlet!*

JOUST

Riding sky bikes while armed with combat clubs – that's all there is to Joust! The aim is to unseat the opponent from the twisting, turning, swerving, rising, falling, rotating bikes.
Points: *10 for unseating the Gladiator, 5 for staying on the bike.*

ATLASPHERES

Caged inside a seven foot diameter metal Atlasphere, contenders have just 60 seconds to steer their spheres into scoring pods. Once hit, the pods emit a dramatic plume of smoke. The only obstacles encountered are two Gladiators, also caged in Atlaspheres and determined to drive the contenders off course!
Points: *3 for each 'score' on a pod.*

DUEL

Armed with a pugil stick and a protective helmet, contenders stand on top of a four foot diameter platform twelve feet in the air. Sixteen inches away is a Gladiator similarly armed. The object is simply to knock them off their perch within 30 seconds!
Points: *10 for a win, 5 for a draw.*

ELIMINATOR

As if all those tough events weren't enough, contenders end the tournament by racing each other over the Eliminator course. The contender who has accumulated most points is given a head start. The course consists of two over and under beams, a twelve-foot rope, a handbike for men, or the overhead ladder for women, a rolling beam, another cargo net, a 90 foot aerial zip line, a balance beam, a treadmill and a swing to the finish line!

GLADIATORS – did you know?

LIGHTNING's favourite lessons at school were PE and art & design. She didn't like history and geography!

The oldest Gladiator is the ferocious **WOLF** who was born in 1952!

HUNTER attended art college for a while. His mum is an artist!

NIGHTSHADE once studied law and sociology!

JET is an avid supporter of the World Wide Fund for Nature!

FALCON's first job on leaving school was as a nanny, looking after a little girl!

SCORPIO supports Fulham FC!

COBRA's favourite lessons at school were history and art!

WOLF has an Anatolian Karabash dog called Tonto. He's a really big dog who takes his master for long walks in the Kent countryside!

The tallest male Gladiator is **WARRIOR**, standing at 6ft 5in. He is also the heaviest, weighing-in at 20st 10lbs!

LIGHTNING was born on Christmas Day 1971.

WOLF was once a table tennis champion in his native Kent, and he even made it into the England squad!

SCORPIO's favourite actor is Klaus Kinski, father of Nastassia!

At 6ft, **NIGHTSHADE** is the tallest female Gladiator!

When she's not in Gladiator costume, **SCORPIO** loves to dress in black!

JET loves to play the flute!

ZODIAC had glandular fever right in the middle of her 'O' level exams!

SARACEN

As far as body-building was concerned, Saracen was something of a late developer. Until the age of 19 he weighed around six stones less than he does today. And even then he only started weight-training to pass the time between shifts in the catering trade! *'I was six feet three inches and really skinny,'* he recalls. *'And I weighed-in at around 11 and a half stones.'*

He really caught the body-building bug after that. He still trains for a least an hour, four times a week, and is an active member of the English Federation of Body-builders.

While working as a professional firefighter, a job which he still does, Saracen also gained some experience in front of the TV cameras. He once doubled for Frank Bruno in a programme about the boxer's life and he appeared in an ITV Telethon. But it was Gladiators which shot him to fame...

Saracen is something of a specialist on The Wall. But his favourite event is Hang-Tough. *'We always follow the women on this event, so the rings are still swinging. That means extra concentration is needed. It's all in the timing!'*

"He's a tough but honorable Gladiator."
Anna Shaw, aged 9, Derby

"He has a job that helps people during the day."
David Cribb, aged 7, Manchester

SARACEN FACTS

Height:	6ft 3in
Weight:	17st 7lbs
Vital Stats:	Chest 46in, bicep 18.5in, thigh 26.5in
Birthdate:	30 August 1963
Starsign:	Virgo
Birthplace:	London
Present Home:	London

IT'S ALL
IN THE
TIMING!

ULRIKA JONSSON

The lovely Ulrika Jonsson, co-presenter of Gladiators, was born in Haggvik, near Stockholm, in Sweden. She first came to England when she was 12-years-old, and already had a command of French, German and English.

Her television career began in a very ordinary way, when she became a secretary at TV-am, a job which obviously instilled in her an ambition to appear in front of the cameras.

After a year behind the typewriter, Ulrika became a production assistant and then a weather girl for SCANSAT, the Scandinavi satellite channel.

It was then that TV-am realised just wh small-screen natural they had let go. They invited Ulrika back, this time as a weather presenter.

The striking Scandinavian beauty soor became a great favourite with the viewers who appreciated her liveliness and her underlying sense of fun. (One morning wh the irrepressible Freddie Starr appeared

the show, Ulrika made an unfortunate slip of the tongue and could hardly deliver her forecast for the day!)

She soon spread her wings and has since appeared in many other programmes, including *Ulrika on the Move*, *6 O'Clock Live* and *Who's Bluffing Who?* She has even been 'gunked' and 'Gotcha'ed' by Noel Edmonds!

But it is as John Fashanu's co-presenter of Gladiators, that younger viewers know her best.

▲ **It's hard to believe that Ulrika once felt unattractive. *'I certainly wasn't in demand with the boys when I was at school,'* she says. *'I had buck teeth and I never once looked in the mirror and said "Wow!".'***

Ulrika really admires the Gladiators team, but reckons she'll never be like them. *'I like to keep fit,'* she says. *'But that would take so much dedication. I think I'll stick to presenting!'*

SCORPIO

"She is beautiful, talented and makes me smile."
John Lowes, aged 5, Pontypridd, Wales

'*Since becoming a Gladiator I've seen many new places and faces and I'm part of a great team,*' says Scorpio. '*These days the sun always seems to be shining in my life.*'

Scorpio's route to Gladiators stardom began in her native Isle of Man where she was brought up and eventually became a conveyancing clerk. '*It was a good job and my colleagues were very nice, but I was restless and wanted adventure.*'

She turned to modelling, a profession which put her off body-building. '*At first I thought having muscles might put people off!*' she remembers. '*But then a couple of photographers encouraged me to carry on with it as it would give me an edge over other models.*'

With a burning ambition to become an actress, she appeared in a number of movies including *Nuns on the Run* which starred Robbie Coltrane and Eric Idle, and she appeared in a rock video with the great Meat Loaf.

Then she read about Gladiators in an article in The Independent newspaper. '*It said that LWT were bringing the American Gladiators to London and were looking for British contenders. I sent my photograph to Nigel Lythgoe who telephoned next day inviting me for an interview. What I didn't know was that I was to be a Gladiator.*'

Ideally, Scorpio would like her role in Gladiators to last forever. '*But all good things seem to come to an end,*' she says. '*So eventually I'd like to be either a TV presenter or play the lead in a sword and sorcery movie!*'

"She's good looking, strong, fierce, but really friendly."
Stephanie Boyd, aged 12, Bray, Ireland

SCORPIO FACTS

Height:	5ft 9in
Weight:	10st
Vital Stats:	40-24-35
Birthdate:	15 March 1965
Starsign:	Pisces
Birthplace:	Isle of Man
Present Home:	West London

THE SUN ALWAYS SEEMS TO BE SHINING!

LIKES AND DISLIKES

Scorpio's favourite event is Hang-Tough. *'It's physically demanding, but very beautiful and visually poetic,'* she says. She admits to a dislike of Atlaspheres. *'I don't like to be caged!'*

I SET THE TREND THAT MOTIVATES THE REST

SHADOW

Shadow used to be a great fan of American Gladiators, but he never dreamed he would become a Gladiator himself. *'Then a friend of mine at a gym pushed me into sending in an application and a photograph,'* he remembers. *'I was interviewed, sent to the try-outs at an army barracks in Woolwich – and then selected as Shadow. Becoming a Gladiator has given me a place in life and has opened doors to other opportunities.'*

Originally, Shadow's ambition was to become an American footballer burning up the astroturf in the NFL. He had caught the gridiron bug as a high-school student in the USA and was a pretty good player who both coached and played with teams in Sweden, France and Germany.

He also excelled at track and field events, particularly the 100 and 200 metres, the triple jump and the shot putt – at which he was school champion.

On leaving school he found a job as a barman at Heathrow Airport. *'And I had a great time doing it,'* he says. But he also pursued a career in body-building, and at the time he posted that letter to Gladiators, he was working as a personal trainer.

Regarded as one of the toughest Gladiators, Shadow says his particular strengths lie in *'my ability to stimulate high octane fuel to all the other Gladiators – I set the trend that motivates the rest of the team.'*

A MESSAGE FOR YOU ALL

Shadow has a special message for all his fans out in Gladiatorland. *'I would like to say a big "thank you" to all my Shadows and Shadowettes throughout the country...I'm watching over you, so listen to The Shadow, be good in school and keep watching Gladiators!'*

"He's kind to children and he tries to hypnotise the contenders."
David and Peter McGarry, aged 7 & 4, Oldham

SHADOW FACTS

Height:	6ft 4in
Weight:	19st
Vital Stats:	Chest 54in, waist 34in, bicep 21in, thigh 30in, calves 18in
Birthdate:	1 July 1961
Starsign:	Cancer
Birthplace:	Kilburn, north London
Present Home:	Worcestershire

"He always wins!"
Michelle Mohieddin, aged 6, Manchester

Gary Mason

Vinny Jones

Oliver Skeets

SUPERSTARS on GLADIATORS

Last year's Gladiators Celebrity Special was full of fun and spectacular action. The Gladiators own John Fashanu came out ahead of boxers Gary Mason and Denis Andries, judo ace Neil Adams, show jumper Oliver Skeets and controversial soccer star Vinny Jones. Our cameras were on hand to snap these great pics.

THE RESULT

Winner:	JOHN FASHANU
Runners-up:	Gary Mason
	Neil Adams
4th place	Oliver Skeets
5th place	Denis Andries
6th place	Vinny Jones

John Fashanu – the winner!

TROJAN

Trojan was quite a sportsman in his teens. A member of the England squash squad, he was ranked in the top twenty Under-19 players in the world. He also represented his district at rugby, javelin, discus and shot and was a county standard American footballer!

His first job on leaving school was as a squash coach in a London gymnasium. *'It was great fun,'* he remembers. *'And I could train all day long!'*

Yet, remarkably, he says he was *'an incredibly shy'* youngster. *'I was pathetically nervous in front of the opposite sex and didn't have a girlfriend until I was 17. In fact, I didn't start to become confident until I started weight-training. I became bigger, stronger and a lot less insecure about myself.'*

Such was the improvement in his confidence and self-esteem, that he later moved to Los Angeles. He was even contemplating becoming a professional body-builder there, but decided to come home when his friend Shadow suggested he should try-out for the 1993 series of Gladiators. *'That was the most nerve-wracking time of my life, but my training paid-off – and my decision to move back to England proved to be the right one when I became Trojan. I became part of a fantastic Gladiators team, and I'll always remember going backstage and being congratulated by Shadow after knocking my first two contenders off the Duel – he taught me how to use the pugil sticks.'*

BODY-BUILDING

Trojan has nothing but good things to say about body-building, the interest which really brought him out of himself as a youngster: *'I've been involved in lots of sports, but can honestly say that body-building is the best! Coupled with a very strict diet – the kind that most other sports don't need – it is the hardest and most disciplined thing I know.'*

Trojan was also selected for the the Powerball 'Dream Team' in the final last year. *'I just love that event – the tackling and the physical contact. It feels great to crush contenders!'*

"He always has a smiley face!"
Daniel Lough, aged 7, Morpeth

"He is strong, handsome and sexy!"
Megan Hassal, aged 9, Sheffield

TROJAN FACTS

Height:	6ft 2in
Weight:	17st
Vital Stats:	Chest 54in, waist 32in, thigh 28in, arm 20in
Birthdate:	25 February 1968
Starsign:	Pisces
Birthplace:	Basingstoke
Present Home:	Central London

I LOVE TO CRUSH CONTENDERS!
Trojan xx

WARRIOR

Remember Warrior in the last series of Gladiators? He was unbeaten in all the individual events, particularly devastating in Powerball and so cool in Tilt that he waved to the audience at the height of the action. *'That was great fun,'* he says. *'But, believe me, I intend to get better than ever in the new series!'* Indeed, the biggest Gladiator is also one of the most competitive.

But then, Warrior has always been that way. As a lad he played football, golf *('I have a five handicap')*, competed in the decathlon, played all racquet sports and excelled at rugby – he was an English Colts Under-19 representative.

Before he was invited along to try-out as a Gladiator, Warrior was training to become a professional body-builder. *'Then I was lucky enough – and good enough – to be chosen as Warrior.'*

These days he trains for four or five days a week, using the excellent facilities of his local football club, Tranmere Rovers.

Warrior's favourite events are the power events, like Powerball. *'My height and weight are my obvious strengths and I use them to my advantage.'*

"He is strong and nobody can beat him!"
Sarah Diamond, aged 10, Tonbridge

"He's big and strong and contenders don't last long!"
Nial Ashton, aged 6, Little Sutton, Cheshire

WARRIOR FACTS

Height:	6ft 5in
Weight:	20st 10lbs
Vital Stats:	Chest 56in, waist 38in, bicep 22in, thigh 31in
Birthdate:	30 December 1960
Starsign:	Capricorn
Birthplace:	St Helens, Merseyside
Present Home:	Birkenhead

I INTEND TO GET BETTER THAN EVER
VULKAN
WARRIOR

"When he doesn't win an event, he gets really mad!"
Ruth Livingston, aged 9, Southampton

"He's mean and mad!"
Ian Deely, aged 10, Halesowen, West Midlands

WOLF FACTS

Height:	6ft
Weight:	15st
Vital Stats:	Chest 48in, bicep 18in, waist 30in
Birthdate:	30 September 1952
Starsign:	Libra
Birthplace:	Bombay, India
Present Home:	Sevenoaks

He's the Gladiator we love to hate...The meanest man on the mat...The referee's nightmare! But Gladiators just wouldn't be the same without the snarling Wolf!

And yet Wolf says he almost didn't become a Gladiator. He had enjoyed a successful career as an actor and also owned a couple of health clubs. *'I was semi-retired,'* he says. *'Then one day a gym member told me he'd heard that the Gladiators were recruiting in Britain. I phoned in, but they said the vacancies had been filled. So, I asked for an application form to be a contender and I sent in a picture and my CV.'*

Soon afterwards the Gladiators production team decided that another recruit was needed after all. *'They rang me for an audition. More than 2,000 applied, and I won a place at the fitness trials – which I excelled in – and the "Wolf" was born.'*

He now considers himself to be *'the fittest over-40-year-old in England'*, when it comes to overall fitness. Yet, because of the success of Gladiators and the many personal appearances he's asked to make, he finds little time for training these days. *'I train maybe once or twice a week – before Gladiators I trained nearly every day.'*

When he does get a chance to work-out, Wolf trains very intensely. *'After a warm-up I do a set of an excerise at 100 per cent, then a second set at 90 per cent. I do two to three exercises per body-part: chest and back, shoulders and arms and legs and calves.'*

In the arena the mean machine just loves winding-up the contenders. *'It was very funny when I pulled the contender's pants down on Hang-Tough,'* he grins.

But even the mighty Wolf has had an embarrassing moment or two of his own. *'The worst was when I lost my balance on Joust – I was nowhere near the contender!'*

It just goes to prove that Gladiators are human, after all!

IT WOULDN'T BE THE SAME WITHOUT HIM!

TV AND FILM APPEARANCES

Wolf has appeared in 15 television commercials, including the role of the Strongman in the Strongbow cider ad. He also appeared in the film *Salome's Last Dance*.

GLADIATORS-AT-A-GLANCE

	FAVOURITE EVENT	LEAST FAVOURITE EVENT	FAVOURITE SPORTS	FAVOURITE TV SHOWS
COBRA	Danger Zone	The Wall	Boxing	*Absolutely Fabulous*
FALCON	Powerball	Tilt	Netball	*Blind Date*
HUNTER	Powerball	Joust	Body-building, judo	*Blackadder, Red Dwarf*
JET	Hang-Tough	Joust	Gymnastics, creative sports	*Absolutely Fabulous, Blackadder*
LIGHTNING	Powerball	Tilt	Swimming, badminton	*Absolutely Fabulous, Roseanne, Barrymore*
NIGHTSHADE	Powerball	Tilt	Athletics, climbing, walking, Tai-Kwon-Do	*Question Time, Big Breakfast*
PANTHER	Powerball	Tilt	Judo	*Brookside*
SARACEN	Hang-Tough	None	Body-building	*The Real McCoy*
SCORPIO	Hang-Tough	Atlaspheres	Athletics, gymnastics	*M.A.S.H., Star Trek*
SHADOW	Powerball	Tilt	Athletics, American football	*Wildlife and undersea programmes*
TROJAN	Powerball	Tilt	Body-building	*One Foot in the Grave*
WARRIOR	Powerball	Hang-Tough	Golf, rugby, soccer	*Sports programmes and true life documentaries*
WOLF	Hang-Tough	Atlaspheres	Snakeboarding	*Star Trek*
ZODIAC	Skytrak	Joust	Pole vaulting	*What's Up Doc?, True Crimes*

FAVOURITE MOVIES	FAVOURITE MALE SINGERS	FAVOURITE FEMALE SINGERS	HOBBIES	FAVOURITE FOOD
In the Line of Fire, Cliffhanger	Smokey Robinson, James Brolin	Whitney Houston	Cinema, cycling	Pizza, cheesecake
The Fugitive	Depends on my mood		Cinema, reading, walking	Pizza
Jurassic Park	Joe Cocker	Aretha Franklin	Eating out, cinema, seeing friends	Italian
Into the West, In the Name of the Father	Johnny Gill, Phil Collins, Guns 'n Roses, Mozart, Debussy	Aretha Franklin	Music, good films, languages	Chinese
The Bodyguard	Meatloaf, Take That	Bonnie Tyler, Tina Turner	Pool, cinema, theatre, TV	Chicken, broccoli and potato pie in white sauce
Demolition Man, Made in America	Ragga, swing beat, and soul		Cinema, meals with friends	Rice, peas and chicken – Jamaica style!
All Good Men	Michael Bolton	Maria Carey	Reading, videos, sunbathing	Pasta, curry
An American Werewolf in London	Most soul artists		Body-building	Fried chicken
Schindler's List	Guns 'n Roses, Meatloaf	Tina Turner	Reading, science fantasy, riding	Italian
Shattered	Public Enemy	Tina Turner	Walking my dogs	Italian
True Lies	Bon Jovi, Guns 'n Roses, Def Leppard, Bryan Adams, George Michael	Barbra Streisand	Writing, drawing, music	Cheesecake
Patriot Games	Everything from Pavarotti to the latest rave!		Golf, eating out	Kentucky Fried Chicken
Wayne's World 2	Johnny Gill	Maria Carey	Snowboarding, skating, snakeboarding	Curry
In the Line of Fire	Van Morrison, The Stranglers, Prince	Dina Carrol, Julia Fordham	Athletics, riding, walking, learning new sports	Mexican tacos

ZODIAC

I JUST LOVE BEING A GLADIATOR!

Gladiators is packed with memories for Zodiac. *'I'd always watched Gladiators on TV and knew Tom McNab, one of the trainers on the show,'* she says. *'When I heard that LWT were recruiting new Gladiators, Tom suggested I send in my photo to Nigel Lythgoe. I couldn't believe it when I got through the trials for the live shows and became Zodiac. I then had to undergo another set of trials with Hunter just two weeks before we started filming the 1993 series in Birmingham. Being a Gladiator has given me more self-esteem and confidence. It does wonders knowing that out of thousands of applicants, I was among those chosen to appear on LWT's most popular children's programme.'*

Zodiac says she enjoys so many of the Gladiators events that it is difficult for her to pick a favourite: *'I love being suspended upside-down like a spider on Skytrack...I love sprinting up The Wall – that really gets the adrenalin going! And I can't wait to do Hang-Tough – I didn't get the chance in the last series as I had stitches in my hand.'*

Those are some of the good memories, but surely Zodiac has some bad memories too? *'Yes I do...I suffered from a really bad stomach upset during the first live shows I did at Wembley. And I was extremely confused and embarrassed when I regained consciousness after my collision in Powerball. I was concussed and afterwards the other Gladiators caught me wandering around the hotel corridors!'*

"She is good at The Wall!"
Christopher Gilling, aged 7, Worksop

"She is a very good sport!"
Samantha Thomas, aged 12, Stone, Staffs

ZODIAC FACTS

Height:	5ft 9in
Weight:	9st 12lbs
Vital Stats:	38-26-35
Birthdate:	2 November 1965
Starsign:	Scorpio
Birthplace:	London
Present Home:	Wimbledon

RECORD HOLDER

Zodiac is the current British Women's Pole Vaulting record holder. *'It's a relatively new event for girls,'* she says. *'I took it up at the ancient age of 25 and have retained the British record since 1992.'*

GLADIATORS COMPETITION!

Here's your chance to win one of these fabulous bicycles from Cycleurope in our great easy-to-enter competition.
And for three runners-up there's a chance to win a selection of Gladiators games from Paul Lamond Games.

All you have to do is answer this simple question (the answer to which is in the Annual):

Which Gladiator didn't begin body-building until he was 19?

... and then tell us what name you would choose for yourself (and why) if YOU could become a Gladiator.

U.K CYCLEUROPE

1st Prize

Gladiators bicycle
suitable for younger children

Gladiators racing bicycle
suitable for older children
(similar to one shown here)

Paul Lamond Games

Runners-up Prizes

Complete the entry form below and send it to the address shown, to arrive before Monday 1 May 1995.
Send a photocopy if you don't want to cut the page.

- The reader sending the first correct entry drawn on 1 May 1995 will win a boy's or girl's bicycle from Cycleurope, matched to the winner's age.
- Three runners-up will each receive a selection of Gladiators games from Paul Lamond Games.

The publishers reserve the right to vary the prizes available, subject to availability at the time of judging the competition.

GLADIATORS COMPETITION

Question: Which Gladiator didn't begin body-building until he was 19?

Answer: ....

If I could become a Gladiator, the name I would choose would be:

....

I would choose this name because:

....

Your name ....

Age .... Your height (to determine frame size of bicycle) ....

Address ....

....

.... Postcode ....

Send your entry to:
Gladiators Competition
Editorial Department
Egmont Publishing Ltd
PO Box 111
Great Ducie Street
Manchester M60 3BL

Don't forget the closing date:
- *Monday 1 May 1995*
- *Send a photocopy if you don't want to cut this page*